The Osprey Suicides

3/15/80

For Peter Stitt,
one of the great good
readers, who labors
with love...

with admiration
and affection,
Larry

The Osprey Suicides

POEMS

Laurence Lieberman (signature)

LAURENCE LIEBERMAN

Collier Books · New York, New York

Collier-Macmillan Publishers · London

ACKNOWLEDGMENTS

Grateful acknowledgment is made to the editors of the following publications for permission to reprint many of the poems in this volume: *Audience Magazine*, *The Hudson Review*, *Jeopardy*, *Modern Occasions*, *The Carleton Miscellany*, *New Orleans Review*, *The Paris Review*, *Quarterly Review of Literature*, *Saturday Review*, and *The Yale Review*. "Huntington Beach" appeared in the Winter 1965 issue of *The Colorado Quarterly*. "Hotel Morgue of Miami Beach" appeared in the Summer 1964 issue of *The Literary Review*. "The Osprey Suicides" appeared originally in *The New Yorker*. "Lobsters in the Brain Coral" appeared in *Poetry*. "Scissors," copyright 1966 by *Shenandoah*, reprinted from *Shenandoah*: The Washington and Lee University Review with the permission of the editor.

The Macmillan Company
866 Third Avenue, New York, N.Y. 10022
Collier-Macmillan Canada Ltd., Toronto, Ontario

The Osprey Suicides *is also published in a hardcover edition by The Macmillan Company.*

Library of Congress Catalog Card Number: 72-87164

First Collier Books Edition 1973

Printed in the United States of America

For Carla, Deborah, Isaac

Contents

I. *Skin-Flying into the Storm Center*

The Diving Ballet

(*for Binnie*)

No one
Can teach us the deep-water
Moves—we are swimming a dance to music
We cannot hear in our heads.
We hear

With our skins.
Holding hands to keep from drifting
Apart, we try to embrace. We brush lips.
But a nearer thing than each
Other,

A kissing
Of many skins, is wrenching
Us out of our two-ness. In water suspended,
Our bodies are inside and out
Of themselves.

As I fall,
You rise. It is a diving
Ballet. Above, you break surface. Below,
Leaning to stay down,
I touch

Bottom—
Thinking, can this be earth?
I am flying so close to a floor whose one
Will is to send me back, feet
First, to a ceiling

Of wind.
I resist, dreaming myself

Empty; weightlessness holds like an anchor.
Now overhead, motionless,
You shadow me,

Belly-floater!
Instantly, you lunge, tumbling—
Taken by impulse, you are set free in your body,
Head flung back, back-
Somersaulting

In a long arc,
A slow-rolling lyric sweep.
As I rise below you, I see in your upside-
Down face curving up to me,
Circling

Up from under you,
The adventure your body, newly
Strange, is beginning to believe in, in
Love with itself. For minutes,
You do not breathe.

You see in,
Looking out. Something within you
Is swimming beyond, getting further ahead
The more slowly it strokes.
Your mind

Must slow down
To catch up. In spaces between
No-breaths, you are learning to hear the waves
Of your pulse cross the Self-
Abyss.

Lobsters in the Brain Coral

Freediving thirty to forty feet, only a few seconds
        to spare
at the bottom of each dive before the death
        of my wind, I catch sight of an antenna or front leg-
            pincer
waving listlessly into the light like a weed-stalk:

        the only visible appendage of a tough old bull langouste,
his spiny-thorned carapace of back wedged deep
        into a crevice in steep flat near-vertical planes of
            rock.
His trench lightless, I can only guess his position—

        impossible to snare him with a gig-noose, I aim the
            Hawai-
ian sling spear, stretched taut on the bow of my forearm.
        The spear connects, freezes. I hustle to the surface for
            air,
hyperventilate, and dive again; hanging upside down,

        my legs dangling over my head, I peer deeply into the
            cleft.
No sign of life. Hah!—he's braced for the fight.
        Tugging and tugging at the spear, I yank out his twenty-
            pound
impaled barrel-shell, his crotchety long legs

        wriggling—he looks like a Gargantuan subaqueous spider!
He contracts his muscular powerful tail,
        discharging high-pitched cries that seem to emit
from a sphere of sound surrounding him, a queer

        distancing remove between the creature and its shrieks.
I compress the tail. He silences. The spear

5

runs deep into his back, diagonally. I force the point,
flared-open within him, through to the other side

and unscrew the spearhead, his great armored body-vault
shuddering quietly. Astonished by his suffering,
        his austere beauty, I relax my grip—he jerks loose,
scraping his backspikes across my bare wrist,

        three streaks inscribing my skin. *The red ink smears,*
runs, thinning off into swirls, a spreading
        stain. Slow leaks—painless—from my punctured inner
                tubes,
I deflate. Oh stop, precious flow. A blowout,

        I may go flat, caving-in on my bones. The lobster zooms
backwards, his tail flapping—violent, noiseless—
        his body, a single bony claw swiftly clenching, unclench-
                ing,
his whines, a siren wailing softer in the distance.

        In pursuit, I chase him below a massive brain coral. I
                swim
under a grayish bulge and drift into the interior,
        my hand gripping the rim. Am I staring inside somebody's
dream? In five or six rooms of his skull—

        sockets like sinuses, honeycombing the coralhead—stand
lobsters of all sizes: some upside-down,
        others on the walls, the floors; always in the dark
corners, favoring the shadows, leaning away

        from the light, antennae waving. I move my glove
to the nearest cubicle and tap a pincer.
        It falls from the body. The lobster drops out of sight
into a hidden channel. Then, the whole colony

        moves in unison: bodies uplifted, legs stretched taut,
unbending, all begin sidling in a slow trot
        around the linings of the caverns, a dance of skinless
bones, creakless many-jointed rickety stilts

6

dragging the glossy-plated bodies this way and that,
somersaulting over and over, sagging
        without letting go, until I forget if my feet are under
or over my head. Let me out of your brain,

        I command the dreamer. I suffocate in this airless hive
where I lose my mass in your sleep. Awake!
        My weight drifts, fades to a gas in your mind.
Do I decompose? *You become an enamelled box*

        on spindly crutches. Lay out your fingerprints length-
                wise
and braid them into two feelers—antennae.
        Fly backwards, snapping your whip of tail; your tail,
the one muscle, the one hatchery, the one edible.

        Wail, if attacked. When cornered, back to a wall,
drop off your legs, twiggy stick by stick,
        flop in the gravelly bottom-muck, a glum squat egg,
quadruple amputee. A basket case. Give me back

        to my jails of skin, to my soaps of blood-suds, to my
                glands,
lungs and lymphs, to all those emerald birds—
        heart, liver, gall bladder and balls. Oh spheres and
                cubes
of my body, multiply strangely into diamonds

        whose many shining stars are eyes, eyes that glow,
eyes that radiate light but admit no spark—
        eyes luminous, eyes opaque—a universe of eyes sparkling
in another's dream. Eyes of my flesh, restored!

Flying Below Sea Level

After hours under water, a mask
        for face,
            air is a ceiling,
and sky a comfortable myth,
            like heaven.
                Sun, a film
of white-hot molten light,
        floats
            on the surface,
like oil. It will scald my scalp
            if I rise—
                to get my breath.
Here and there, planes of light
        intersect
            the surface, knife
the upper field, and fan out
            in shelves.
                In shallows, they strike
bottom, spilling rainbow
        all about
            the coral. There
are brains in the fish's tail
        (alert
            for messages), the fins
are nerves, each scale a fingertip . . .
            My cheek,
                slapped by a moulded
soft-spongy mass, half-moon
            shaped—
                gently stinging—
I dodge a gelatin-trio, running
            with the current
                faster than I can
swim away. Then, I'm surrounded

8

by hordes,
        mounds bumping
each other, sliding around me—
        painless
            between my legs,
across my face. Wherever I
        look, the sea
            is milky-translucent,
separate outlines no longer
        visible.
        The water, gelling
into a vast slug-slimy pudding—
        impenetrable—
            half-carries me along
(a man-blob swallowed in viscid
        ooze), half-
            disgorging me,
by turns. I dive, down-thrust
        through a hole
            opening just under
me, swim below the flying island
        of jelly,
            and enter the under-
water cave. I hear a high-pitched
        crackling,
            like dry twigs
burning, on all sides enclosed
        by a soundless
            hush. I hang,
motionless, at the center of the cave:
        magnetized . . .
        I am seen
by thousands of unseen eyes!
        I shudder
            at a burst of color:
a large hogfish, bright scarlet-
        orange, appears;
            high-finned, majestic,

9

wide and flat, brilliant-sheened;
seeming twice
its size, swelled
in enclosure. No change in his wide-eyed
elongated
hog-snout at sight
of me, no change in his glide-rhythm,
he picks up
speed as he spins,
circling the interior of the cavern;
so nervous
to escape me, he misses
the exits, tunnels, again and again.
The space
around me expands.
Light from no source filters up
from depths
without bottom.
I grow larger and larger. The cave
I filled
fills me. As I wind,
snake-easeful, back through the cave-
mouth, I
feel the whole sea
tilt to fill the missing space.

Flying on the Surface

Aloft on the unpunctured float
Of lungs and flipper-rubber,
I thread the needlefish with my spear, a snorkeling
Headhunter: the gar leading
With pointed nose,
Two interlocked

Rows of teeth, saw-edged,
That can cut a brother
In two—the decapitated head snapping blindly
At whatever passes before it,
Long after the severed
Body has fallen

Away: needlefish javelins
Streaking after fry,
Targets themselves for swooping birds: one gar, struck
By a gull divebomber—instantly
Disembowelled—
Dies, a still live

Minnow in its mouth. My forehead,
Submerged, konks
The feet of a snoozing pelican, listless, drooping
Discarded knotty branches
Near the raft
Of his broad bottom,

Shading eleven small squids
Back-jetting in an undulant
Double-V formation: a sine wave motion, ribbon-
Winding from end to end.
I jab at the middle
Link: it spurts

Three feet ahead of the chain,
But divides in two,
Splits—no, doubles!—leaving an inky-black pseudomorph
In its place, impaled round
My spearpoint, thinning
To a smoke-ring. Near

Stumpy Point, where bay-mouth
Meets open sea,
Breakers converging from three sides at once, mixing
And chopping their flows, reinforcing
Or cancelling by turns—
I slip in shallow

Water, yellowtail on my spear.
Juggling gunshaft
And spear in one hand, unsheathed knife in the other,
Unbalancing on one leg
In two feet of water—
I'm struck from behind

By a six-foot wave I didn't
Hear building over me
From the left, the wave silently purring a surf-lip
As the crest curls down in a fist
Of foam—to pounce
With cat's stealth: I hear

A cracked-whip's impact before I
Recall it is my side
And neck that echo back; taste blood in the salt
Before I know my lifestream
The one opened, and on
The run—escaping

Smoothly as into a love-sucking
Mouth; see a black fin
Slicing the surface and circling toward me before I
Register the terror-sound

Of flippered feet
Wedging between coral

Jaws to brace the mindless
Trunk they swing upon
        Absently, my legs a lever, bending against the back-
            Wash of the wave's undertow
                Pulling seaward to meet
            A next hammering wave.

        Shark-meat! Half-aliveness will eat
You alive! On all fours,
        I scramble ashore. . . . Now in dreams, I sink into brain-
            less
            Stupor, a carcass emptied
                Of self, a drifting
            Deadwood, a flotsam

        Of absent flesh: my legs two
Shanks of floating
        Sea-fodder, my arm-bones crossed sticks under a death's-
            Head skull, my eyes looking
                Out through a death
            Mask of face.

Whelk Hunter in the Staghorns

In the low tide,
heavy surf batters the natural breakwater forest
                    of antler coral, thousands
                    of many-jointed crisscrossing arms
                    reaching above
        the briny surface, absorbing
shock after shock,
shielding my suicidal roosts—an occasional high-lipped
                    breaker overtopping the stag-
                            horns—
            as I pick my way between
            low inshore coral
    ledges, scouting for whelks.

A mere seven-footer
is a killer wave here, thinks the human crab, crawling
                    on ice-slick shelves, terraces
            of stone, creeping and paddling
            by turns as the water
        level rises and falls.
Knees and forearms
slipping on the flat-topped silkmossy rocks of the inlet—
                    half sizzling in the bake of
                        sun,
            half awash in foam—I dodge
            the exposed horns
    of dozens of coral elks:

Sea-moose! My eyes
fastened to my wavering footholds, as I stalk, catpawing
                    from footing to delicate foot-
                        ing;
            my neck in a half-twist, I take
            nervous side-glimpses

of the far-to-near oncoming waves,
but my eyes fail:
they miss the signals, the worst wave hiding its froth-curl
                              in the undersea ground swell.
              I must learn to hear the hiss
              and suck of the undertow,
          to feel in my shanks the least

tug of the backsliding
shallows, to sniff and detect fear-smell as it wafts
                              from my epidermal radar:
              All warning systems alert!
              The water below
          my rest shelf sinks dead away;
I follow the least
trickles of wet seeping into bottom-mud craters,
                              and the gliding shadow looms
              overhead. *I must cling like a leech*
              or be dashed to a pulp,
          my belly flat to a wide stone
slab, my four limbs,
crab-claws, hooking around the spiny ledges, tucked under,
                              my back braced for the churn-
                                      ing
              blow. . . . After the wave passes,
              I continue to clutch
          the boulder, pressing my gut
into the lifelines of stone,
sensing in each rock-ripple millennia of water-carved
                              intricacy. Slowly, I begin
              sliding forward, all my life
              flowing into my belly,
          my back, strangely emptied,

toughening into a senseless
rind—all one piece—a curved bone-plate like the univalve
                              shell of a whelk or conch. . . .
              Hugging the coastline, I swim out
              from enclosed bay-mouth
          over deeper water beside shore

cliffs: flat slabs,
sheer planes of rock-face, steep walls of natural dikes,
                            No footholds or handrests
                            here.
                    No arm-lifts for swimmer, weary
                    or seeking hideaway
            from shark. No narrow trails

for shore-rats, mongoose,
iguana. A barrenness not to be scaled by wild rock-cling-
        ing
                            vines: no earth deposits
                    for climbing-ivy shoots—
                    tough, leafless,
            and rubbery-flexible—to take root.
Firm lodgement only
for quick-scurry lives, all crack dwellers: shellfish,
        creepers
                            of pit and rock-pocket; trig-
                            ger-quick
                    land crabs, soft-bodied, light,
                    exquisitely poised
            on legs that can tighten their grip

on stone sheer as glass,
rocking up-and-down, quavering: most skilled amphibian!—
                    nimble-kneed land crab, strad-
                    dler
                    of rock, wind and wave—loving
                    to survive on the edge,
            perched for the breaker's chop.
Or rock-sucking whelk,
sliding just over or under the waterline, stranded
                            too high on rock ledge if
                            the tide
                    recedes too fast, becoming fixed:
                    frozen to a grave
            by sundried salts: tiny rock-knob!

Moles in the Whelk Nest

Along the sides
of a coral-wall, many shells kissing the falling waterline
                    abruptly emerge, sliding upward.
                    I can hardly believe their numbers.
                    Careless of injury,
          I leap into ten-foot-deep water
hunting the source.
Moiling plankton and bubbly froth-clouds block my underwater
                    sight. My gloved hands probe
                    and slither along sandy contours.
                    Eyes in my hands.
          Mind's-eye in my fingertips. Drop off,
gloves. Fear.
Fear of sea-urchin spines. Long black needles that sink
                    deeply into flesh, break off,
                    leave irremovable splinters,
                    dissolve slowly
          for months. Much pain. Swelling.
My fingers searching,
fondling the slime, threading through eelgrass and moss,
                    sensitive to textures, to smallest
                    faults or clefts. *Fingers stroking*
                    a woman's fine hair,
          the sides of the fingers—not only
the tips—learning
the kinks, the flowing tress-silk. Deciphering in love-dark
                    the stiff single gray hairs
                    from the resistless soft blondes
                    and browns. Caressing
          the coarse bristly hank of curls
over the genitals,
as springingly alive to the touch as flesh; or the soft
                    thin down on the rim of the ear,
          the earlobes. My knuckles gouging

into pits and sockets,
wedging into interstices of the reef,
tracing lineaments
and burrowing into all declivities. My hands tunnelling
like underwater moles, hunting
orifice—the aperture into secret
wombs of the coral.
At last, my left hand drops
into a deep hollow
taking my arm in behind it to just over the elbow and lands
on a close-knit pile of rocks:
roundish pebbles, stacked one
on two or three
others, spreading out downward
in a pyramid, the bottom
layers containing larger—the upper layers, smaller—ovals.
Whorls and spirals of my fingerprints,
think for me! Note finely etched ridges,
wavelike crests,
at short intervals, elevated
on the surface. Ah!
Familiar shapes. I have invaded the secret nest of the whelks,
a family of shells in luxuriant
embrace, a community of mollusks
all connected,
lip to back, content in a multi-
leveled architecture.
I start prying. As if drugged, they spring up into my hands
loosening in threes and twos, oilily
slurping together—now lip to lip—
as they fall into my net.
The nest runs deep as a lode
of metal ore,
I, a blind miner, with bare fingers for shovels and picks,
knuckles for sledgehammers: the meat
in my skullcase, my ribshell meat,
my gutbag—all hungering
for the gummy wormmeats of the whelks!

Peacock Flounder

A patch of sandy bottom shifts left,
halts, backs up. It's flapjack.
                                        I give chase,
stamp each last place the sand jumped too late.
I slip, fall backwards, cup him under
my instep.
                    Flapjack's underside, turned
up in my hand, is dirty near-white:
his former right side, now his bottom, it
always faces down. When two weeks young,
flapjack leant on his side; liked to lie
low and swim flat; stayed turned, left side up.
His eyes, on independent swivels,
stare oppositely, at each other
perhaps (both on topside), or off two
ways. The underside eye (old right),
the rover, migrated to topside
when flapjack switched from upright to side-
lying posture.
                    I study his top
side (old left), pancake-flipped on my hand
griddle: a peacock pattern of blue
spots, neon-winking in large gray-green
dark rings, the colors altered to fit
whatever tones the background, from sand's
nocolor to coral's varicolor,
takes, chameleon-quick.
                                I release him.
Floor-scudder!
                    —he drops, plumb to the bottom,
scoots a few feet, shivers, throwing sand
over his back (topside), roots in, half
burying himself.
                    He hugs his flat-
ness to the sameness underfoot . . . Blends.

Skin-Flying into the Storm Center

Wary of lightning,
we dodge the thundercloud's blue-black
center—the sky overhead pulsating feeble glimmers—
swimming across the current to escape
the heavy drift tugging us back
into the gray storm-patch.
We are alert for the whirring
steel propeller knives of the
French
fishing skiffs, their skippers
dozing; to the ear of a submerged diver,
the whine of the outboard
motors is a power mower in the distance,
up close an electric handsaw: we hug the surface!
A quartermile downcurrent, a tall vertical
flickering shadow appears—
too low for a cloud.
We make our meteoric flashes
of white against sky's pearlgray,
blurred swirls of activity.
We are pulled nearer. Zigzagging traceries
become arcs of tails
and wings twirling like leaves
in a wind-whipped elm: a flock of gulls and frigate birds,
packed so thick they block out light
like a storm-cloud, chasing
vast schools of fish.
We swim closer, closer.
Needle-beaked streaking darts!
The frigate birds, streamlining
their forked scissorstails, nosedive for fish.
Now bird-beaks whiz
past my ear, just under my mask-
glassed nose. A sword-blade plunges before my eyes,

trailing a beady-eyed undersized ball peen
head, tail feathers vanishing;
the reversed sword emerges
tipped over, gliding hori-
zontally: it skims the surface,
dragging a wildly convulsive
high-backed king mackerel, twice the length
and weight of its captor.
Remarkably, the beak dismembers
the backflesh and swallows without loosening its iron-
clamp grip.
From all sides, a dozen-odd gulls attack,
stripping clean the exposed fish-
skeleton, while the helpless
carrier-bird makes futile
sideways dashes to escape,
unable
to salvage any gob of its prey.
Many gulls thwack into the carcass with furor,
the lifeless fish quaking
more violently than when it gave up
its last life-spasms to the single killer beak—still holding
firm, despite the simultaneous concussion
of numerous rivals striking
the same last traces
of meat-flakes from bones.
Voracious, they seem to aim
for each other's necks and skulls,
but zeroing in from all angles—even below—
each hits the mark.
A sharkfin cuts through the slaughter-
bloodied rainbow sea. Flipper-flapping madly, we lunge
from the murky bloodlake into crosscur-
rents.
Swiftly, we are taken by four knots
of current—holding our arms
and legs like rudders, we learn
to keep steady, steering a few
degrees

against the mainstream
like sailboats tacking into the wind. Now we pass
directly into the eye
of the storm. We sense the current
reversing—a few strokes further—without surface signals.
Just ahead and below, I see fish lean
sharply
at an angle, or am *I* turning
sideways? Now the fish
lie flat on their sides,
struggling back up, to turn
upright,
but falling away. . . . Suddenly,
we are stunned by stillness—a deep hush in the air.
We are motionless.
The absence of current is chilling . . .
Skin sleeps. Air is a vacuum to us. When the wind
blows, do we think, air-thick: *it is this*
we take in and puff out each moment
of life? With this
we ignite the calories,
burning them to bones and brains!
Listen. *Her appetites*
will never be satisfied. She is wife of the storm
and mother to capricious
gusts. Too thin to melt,
too fine to cut a petal, this chaste pool's elusive.
Her issue can choke a whale, hew mountains,
reverse the pattern of seas
and continents.
She files her teeth on shale.
But the skin sleeps, won't touch
her fierce invisible waves. . . .
Slosh, slosh—all at once the rain floods
down on our heads.
In fear of drowning, absurdly,
we drop masked faces in the sea. Just under the surface,
preternatural blue-gray stillness! Above:
fingers of ice run over
our necks and backs.

Pure salt-free taste. A solid
                    rainwall gushing froth, a surf-
                    floor
everywhere continuous:
    cold, density, rage and blindness. . . .
Below: warmth,
airy thinness, ghostly calm.
    Crystallinity to all depths: every particle glint-edged,
                striated with color; all angles and curves
                        of minutiae insistent to the eye,
                disseveral. Allseeingness!
    Incandescence! The self—
                        a luminous subterranean eye—
        spreading like sight, radiating
    hundreds of feet in all directions from the storm
        center.

The Spearing

Who am I chasing—underwater—in my life?
When I spear a fish in the face,
Do my own eyes
Stare back
As the life rushes out?
My best friend's eyes? Or my wife's?
Is the wish to see pain I make in the face

Of a loved one akin to murder? Does the blood
In my erection leave blood on my hands?
Are you in love with
My death
Of you? When we cook
The fish, do you eat the eyes?
They will stab you, just under the heart.

Why do you *eat* so much? Swollen and massive,
A great Jewfish, do you turn
Your back to me
All night
And wait to be skewered,
Looking behind with fantastic
Puffy face? When I dived for the lovely

Pompano—with majestic jutting head—
You looked after me 'til I spun
Out of sight, spiralling
Down—Oh
I went too deep,
And something burst in my head
Like a grenade as I kicked to the surface,

But my eardrums walled out the blast. At night,
You tickled your love in my ears,
Talking and purring

It would be
All right. By morning,
I was stone-deaf, your tongue
All spotted with blood, a lover's knife.

II. *Increasing Night*

Increasing Night

His empty heart is full at length,
But he has need of all that strength
Because of the increasing Night
That opens her mystery and fright.

—W. B. Yeats

I get closer to the dream, trying to remember
What happened and to learn which of the accidents outside
Became parts of my urgent inner life,
When my attention lags and the wrong lines

From a beloved somebody else's trouble invades my page—
Whose heart's occlusions usurp my heart's—
And all my tongue's wrestlings and wranglings to translate
The flames of my dream's furnace

Into mirroring music are hopelessly garbled.
The great effort with which I rage to forget Love
And Lord are my stubbornest lies to outsmart is stupidly
Heroic, for all my crimes of loving

And sins of prayer are a pale cover-up
For the ear's guilt of deafness to the dream's call,
For the mouth's guilt in turning away
From sleep's lips kissing the brain awake,

For the hand's guilt in absentmindedly (but never acciden-
        tally,
There are no accidents!) relaxing its grip,
Breaking the vision's handshake, dropping the mountaineering
Twin brother-in-the-spirit

Headlong on his daily plunge to the death
From the precipice of waking

29

Into the bottomless gulch of irrecoverable ghostlife,
The secret life I am overkind to friends

Falsely every day to forget I am failing, the failed
Dream all my success unsuccessfully hides
Or numbs until sleep
The incorruptible arsonist (just try to bribe

Or buy *him* off, just try!) sets fire
To no matter how many faces I've donned and doffed
In losing battles with the permanent mask spreading
Like cancer-blooms under my selfafraid eyes.

Frozen Pipes

Pipefreeze! Pipefreeze! "Thaw the ice-clots. Stop house-
        stroke!"
                the plumber warns, murmuring
    with a voice like running water into the receiver's
earpiece. His speech is alkaline, his advice a wordy Drāno
            licking clean the telephone wire's
        bad plumbing: "No time for house calls. Fix it,
yourself."
                    Five days of ten below, five gelid nights!
                Our tube-fed furnace sips
            from underground pools of natural gas.
    The many vent-grids, louvered mouths in the walls
            of each room, keep breathing
        a small hot failing puff, the long sigh
from the floorvent riffling my trousers and blond leghairs
        like a panting hound. I hear
    the dry click of ice upon ice, as three
new stillborn births abort from the automatic
        icemaker into the bucket below,
        each rotating set of triplet-cubes
    perfectly formed (how painless to be born into death
            before life—frigid and flawless!)
    for chilling our drinks to the immortal fixed temp
of freezing and melting.
                        In a recurring dream of my father,
            who died last fall when the frozen
        pipe burst in his heart, I try to fathom
    the outrageous quantity of heat that is stolen from life
            when ice melts to freezing
        iced water with no change in temperature. . . .
That lummox, the icemaker, keeps dropping its quota of babies—
        thousands of unfertilized fisheggs—
        while surplus icecaviar is frosting the windows,
    icicling the eaves, and crystallizing the steam of anyone's

              outdoors breath into minutest
    hail.
                The frostbiting vapors are leaking
through doorjambs, through cracks in windowframe caulking—
    all
           seals in my house's mesenteries,
    all tar paper and clapboard body linings, fail.

Lamb and Bear: Jet Landing

(for Isaac)

    At each level
of jetfall, rougher turbulence:
     my son, in deepest
slumber of engine-drone, drug-limbed,
     nods. I motion to undo
his belt, hesitate . . . *a wind-gust
     could send you flying,
loose egg, across the cabin. . . .*

    When you awake,
if you wish, you can cut me
     in twos, in two
halves, or two mes, your dreamed
     sirs, so gladly
beside you, shining. Do you know,
     my shut lips, if they
could tell, glow. Inside, I am

    who opens up to you.
Unsticking your eyelids, sleep's
     fleece sheering off,
you look at my hands, then yours.
     You concentrate. Soon,
we've exchanged hands, yours
     doubled, mine halved.
You look up—we trade faces,

    not eyes. My son,
if it please you, enter.
     Lean into my
bones. Slide under my skin.

33

Wear me. An old
bear hide, hairy, pot-bellied.
When I wither (I
promise I shall), shed me!

The Killing of Daddy

(for Carla)

Impossible! Where could you hide?
This dwarf slope
The only hill for miles. I saw,
I remember, your face

Be taken by shadow, a darkness that passed
To you in secret
From snowfields, the ghost of grass

Buried in immaculate
Whiteness. The next moment, you fled.

Child, you knew you could hide
In the sheltering light. You felt snowblindness—
A power like nakedness—
Steal from my eyes your body's
Mask of visibility.

Green with panic, I shout
Your name to echoing
Flatness, the white sheets

Of continuous overcast spreading below,
Flowing into distant uplands,
Glare blurring the salience of horizon
To a desert blankness.

I shut my eyes. *Count*
Backwards from one hundred to one. Take
Slow steps, slow
Steps. Stop. Open. Look down.

You are curled in a ball at my feet,
Drunk on wraths
Of concealment. As I bend to touch

Your hair, you shed
Invisibility—sinking into muteness,
A safer distance, deeper. Your silence grown
Perfect, you speak,
The edges of your words arrowheads

Tipped with a poison to end
Your babyhood. Puberty

Seeps into your snowpants from grassroots.
You send me away, killing
A child's daddy. *Heiress, learn husbandry.*

From carrion sire, you may harvest
A young lady's friend.

Inside the Gyroscope

(for Debra)

Daughter, this is our laughing-box:
a gyroscope orbiting us
two ways at once—
top to bottom, left to right. I try to relax
and enjoy the scares, to roll
with the machine's laughing gears—the computerized gentle
terrors, but shock kills my cackles:

I freeze like a funnybone
when the bumped elbow's burning nerve tickles
the length of your arm, and the skin—
pricked with a thousand
pins—tingles. As we sail
through the wider arc of the tilting Great Wheel,
our eggshell cage, an ellipsoid

spinning on its axis, hurtles me
upon you; my weight—
stone in a sling—pinning you sideways against our satellite's
grillewire, your legs tangled under,
frail wings flapping: "Daddy,
you take the steering bar,
give us a rough ride, make us twist

and twist." Now we halt,
trapped in the middle of a reverse somersault,
careening, heels over heads,
rocking on the base of our skulls. We are staring straight
up, fifty feet to the ground,
into three ovoids—family faces—high overhead
and directly below us:

mother and sister O-mouth gapes, the wailing face
of your brother, whose helium
balloon has fallen
up, up, up (I nearly capture the string,
its lifeline, poking
two fingers through the wiremesh
grate) and drops skyward

under our legs, shrinking
to an agate, a green pea, a pinhead
trailing a hair; it sails into a cloud, vanishing. . . .
I waken from a whacky dream. Stepping from bed
in the dark, I slip on the soft
bumps of my daughter's hips and head.
Must I walk on walls to spare her pain? When I lift

her to carry her back
to bed, the chill of the floor
passes from belly to belly. She is winning her war
with sleep—a rage to stay awake!
A little past midnight, she embarks on nocturnal tours:
I hear a soft pitter-patter like a mouse
under floorboards. She cartwheels

from room to room—practices
handsprings, headstands for Saturday tumbling class.
Like a wind-up toy, its spring coiled to the snapping point,
she never unwinds.
She rummages about the great toy-bin
of our house, moony-eyed, alchemizing our leaden nights
into goldened lonely second

days. She never lies down.
Sleep must overtake her in mid-play, standing up.
I find her in odd corners at sunup:
on the second shelf of the linen closet, half-awake,
buried in washcloths, towels; under the sofa,
the face of the lion rug curled over her ear, its sunflower
yellow whiskers licking her cheek.

Love, the Barber

Love, the barber, shaves the night fields.
He trims the forests. Between his blades

Fall waves of the sea. They calm themselves.
Whatever falls away grows back in another

Place, in sleep. Beautiful hanks. My wife
Cuts my daughter's hair. Oh, it hurts my eyes

At first. Sweet face, you look so bare.
The brute has severed locks of sleep, and weightless

Dreams are falling fast, oh fast; the floor
Is strewn with waves of softest curls.

Let us walk there, only if we must. Step
Lightly. What fell from you I lift

In my hands—through stumbling
Fingers slip your thinnest strands.

2.

Love, the barber, eats down to the roots. Clip, clip.
Yes. I swear the air has teeth some nights

And chews the fields, but not from hunger.
Some bites caress the wound, and heal like death. . . .

My students are cropping their long hair shorter,
Not short, lifting just over their once-covered

Shoulders, their necks still hidden. No ears.
Thought, unspoken, waves through the classroom,

39

Curls, and in curling, straightens our backs.
My idea, a tight braid, unties, shakes loose.

We are revising our poems. I can be happy to collapse
Into my lines, the furrowing lines in my forehead.

We lift crooked faces. All together—this moment—
We are growing back our lost features.

The Vanishing Classroom

This room we tremble in together,
Concentrating very hard to remember
    A dream we had yesterday,
Has six walls: the floor and ceiling
So perfectly mirror each other, we cannot
    Tell them apart. Forgetting
Up and down are chances to take, we narrow
Our eyes for a safer squint,

Sighting left to right and right
To left, trapping the whole world
    In sideways vision.
We sit in a circle facing each other.
On good days our friendliness resists
    The room's squareness.
The flat walls arch their backs,
Corners renounce the safety

Of angles for arcs of trust. Our feelings,
Curving clockwise or counterclockwise,
    Go shorter distances
Than straight lines, the next needed impulse
Our only guide. These are rare inklings
    That take us, our tongues
Blessing the medium we float in—
If water, we must be swimming; if air,

Flying—whichever way we turn.
We glide with the freedom of skaters
    Looping figure
Eights with their eyes shut, confident
They often swerve in the same cracks
    Twice, their new moves
Intersecting their old moves—their presents
Their pasts—with enough fear.

Homage to Austin Warren

1. At the Book Sale: A Memory

A leatherette relic smelling of musk and camphor falls

Open in my cup of hands to a zany overmarked
Page: there is
No mistaking the scrawled marginalia of Austin Warren
Crowding the print off the page,

Demanding, insisting, bickering in a kingly true lover's
Tiff over word flesh-and-blood, I am swept
Back into the aura of that raspy
Voice   slow-gurgling   weighted down by tonnage
Of learned reference

Warren's voice—unmistakably no one else's—blazing into
        memory

As I pore over the remarks in a worried
Black script, penned in that familiar, crabbed, near
Illegible hand (whether difficult

From nerves, illumination, or sheer weight of mind

On edge I was never to know)   I recall
I'd chewed for hours like a dog on a pant leg
At obscure marks on themes, some words
Beginning with odd caps placed wrongly   for emphasis
Which one my grade?   Somewhere   I

Guessed   in that barbwire alphabet   the clue to my future

2. In Frontroom Chapel

The summer I first winged words   sent them flying   arrows
Effortlessly zinging   feathered into being . . .

In the apartment upstairs,   I could not seem to open
My eyes wide enough to take
In the foreignness of frontroom chapel   breath-

Drugging incense smoke-curling up from the altar
The crucifixion   between wooden frames
Wire-hung on a bent hook   imperceptibly awry   the wine-
Maroon walls   papered unbrokenly   tier
Upon tier   with oilskin of bookbacks   outspreading
From floor to ceiling

                    who was it   who I
Kneeling at his feet   not in prayer   shakily   who
He   leafing pages of type-
Script   his high forehead scrunching at wrongnesses
Everywhere met   all efforts
To conceal the badness of words his eyes scanned
Failed
Who we   his one voice speaking
For two the sound coming or seeming to come from one point
Above and from another inside my head

Falling out of the room upper air
As out of a cloud

Our bodies   our lives in the present are strange
To us   of all the beings to whose lips he lifted my hands
His selves were the least known   a breath

From Shakespeare's nostrils warmed
My fingertips   there was room for Donne and me to share
Intimacies in Warren's one
Skin of his poems   sentences of Henry James
He spoke inflated the unused ear of my mind like a third lung
          air
Found in my second wind of hearing a better place

To stream   I took one step   from hearing to breathing one
Step   the trained ear flowering into voice
Shaking loose   my own voice   a blossom   opening

43

Rock and Cloud

The man believes the marriage of rock and cloud.
Photo: the cloud, in his hand, lifts
the house over his head,
over the waving arm of his wife
perhaps. The children, on swings, look up

to sea or down to sky. They stay. The horizon saws
off their heads. The downhill-gliding
man, suspended,
beholds. *Negative*: she ascends
in cloud; he sinks into rock. The children

drift upside down in his cloud of going. Tears
fall upward. He lies on his back, now
in the valley. Clouds
black as rock he perceives
are rock. The earth he hears whisper

leans at his temple. Things that would mean to grow
therefrom tilt him upright. He answers
the call, and hearing,
is heard. (Cloud and rock
change faces: distance within absence,

free space and mass, mix.) A sphere of light
starts between two shelves of cloud.
It starts from her eyes
and entwines the children's arms,
their faces and hands aglow. *Overexposure*:

Light overflows, now pouring downhill, flooding into
the man—whatever is rock within him
is floating away,
dissolving to light, to cloud.
Rock, cloud-white, *is* cloud. *Is light.*

Song of the Thrush

In terror of my typewriter's greed for profit,
Tethered to business letters
Bleeding out of my hand, I hasten, a guest
Trespasser my beckoning neighbor

Halts, half out of my clothes half in, my face coloring
Before I can think *shame*, how much of me is showing

I cannot check now, but I feel cool
In two or three wrong skin
Places. Decoyed, I quit the public walk,
Prancing to the lawn, obedient

To her pointing finger, her lips including me in a message
I cannot hear over traffic, her husband beside her

Sighting directly on a branch at eye-level
Tail feathers: the first thrush
Of spring. Oh happy transport! I'm severed
By a cadence from the ambition magnet

Pulling my letters to the corner mailbox. Her face
Wound in its mystery, her arms folded for warmth

In the morning chill shift to a cradling
Motion as she explains how
Important the thrush music was each morning
Last spring when the nursing baby

Woke her at four. The thrush rescued her from petty
Anger, lifted her spirit, and deadened the worst

Acids of postpartum orneriness, her fifth
Offspring a boy at last,

Their last try taking more nerve than hope
After twin girls. Both past thirty-five.

Both saved. It is a joy to them for me to share their plunder
Of the bird they love. I bow to charities of the thrush.

Dragons in the Subway

1. *Faces*

On the wrong subway at three o'clock in the morning,
afraid to go out into an obscure part of an unknown
town, fearful to stay on with the shifty-eyed men
and the sensual women, the bewildering flux of races,
such beauties of skin, such poise of carriage, bodies
with rhythm and grace, and the suave treasures of faces,
some mashed to a featureless dough, a drab flatness,
others carved to splendor of contour and shapeliness,
myself gawky and, for the moment, exalted, struggling
not to stare into faces that are what they feel
and feel what they are, this him with a hundred masks,
this mole that burrows through obsidian layers of self—
soft-bellied, ink-witted, toothy, dragging his shyness
behind him like a clubfoot, can find no face of his own.

2. *The Dragon*

I have come underground. It seems
the air is thin. It will not be cool.
One may as well breathe fire.
It will do no harm. It may be to have a soul.
And the flames are fun to share.
With *you*. Haven't we met, in dreams?

It is hard to walk with a tail
that drags, but mine is light. It waves.
And no one is puzzled. Or scared.
If I were a tree no one would notice my leaves.
It is marvelous. But people are bored.
I itch. I wonder how bad I smell.

Sometimes I race the trains.
I try to hear their heartbeats. They are lonely.

47

They cannot cry when it hurts,
and I'm sure it does. I tell them: "Tears are manly.
Don't you believe in spirits
of the dead? I do. They sleep in my bones."

On the trains, I act polite.
I put out my flames and try not to blow
smoke into anyone's face.
There are so many kinds of people, I fit in too.
And the people-bodies are nice
to touch. I may be not a Jew. Or White.

Party at the Embassy

1

The faces were unfamiliar.
Still worse, the talk. Sunglasses
were less than no protection from prying

voices. But I would hide
my eyes to keep out the foreign
stares. And I thanked God for Myra, that she was

my wife. At the party, girls.
But their children would be of different
races. The lips I touched were paste. And kisses

were waxen. So I swallowed my ice
and opened the other cases.
Into the glasses. The bottles were filling up faces.

2.

Myra was warming up. Al-
ready she was dancing with somebody
else. But she promised! The faces were filling up

wider and wider spaces.
She promised her kisses. Once
a bitch, always . . . always I wished for her kisses.

My wishes were poison. I hardly
could see, for the faces and stolen
kisses, what she was doing or who she was doing it

with. I stretched my neck
to see, and saw in the bottlenecks.
There were oblong heads that bobbed over severed necks.

49

And some of the oblong faces
rested on necks intact. But they
wobbled and seemed to be broken. My voice, in the bottle,

was muffled. I spoke in bubbles.
Myra was hissing. Her tongue
was long and narrow. But it would not fit in the bottle.

I couldn't stand. I thought I
was getting sick. *The faces*
were filling up bottles. Her tongue was pointed, but wouldn't

fit. My neck was stuck. She
was upside down in the bottle. They
were dancing, and her eyes were swimming faster

than the faces, and I
hoped to Hell he wouldn't.
My teeth were charred. I was twisting on a spit.

The Guest

Two who had loved in each other's eyes met strangeness.
Wonder at loss. Distance. It seemed as if

(we pondered alike) a third party, a guest,
who knew us both, and lived, or seemed to live,

in our relation (shadow), grew as we grew,
suffered what gave us pain and breathed our breath

of ardor, had grown between us like a thorn.
An apartness. Or lifted (perhaps) subtly and secretly

away, as a feather in a light wind, a thistle
disengaged. . . . In our eyes, knowledge of loss.

Wonder at absence. Vacancy. Terror at peace,
at acceptance—easy adjustment to unspeakable emptiness.

Scissors

So busy trying to say something, but unable to convey it,
    must you always *cut in?*

And those powerful jaws of yours—they bite into leather or
    paper
    with the same dull force.

Open and shut. Open and shut. There is only one way to move.
    And if you destroy,

You do so from the innocent wish to express yourself—chomp,
    chomp.
    I distrust your friendship:

The way you meet newness is to snip off a sample for flavor.
    Bite
    first. Ask questions later.

Like lips, you suppose you bless whatever you touch, with
    or without reverence,

Or that your constant agitation is necessary as labor pains,
    or the beating of wings,

And wherever you sink your teeth you expect to get to the
    heart
    of the mystery. And promptly.

Your brother, the knife, is more punctual, clean and exact.
    He knows more of death.

Death would be neat and orderly, without commotion. A saint-
    liness.
    And death strikes once.

There is no ungainly shuffling of moving parts. No hysteria.
    No jagged, frayed edges.

Swift as intention and deep as old pain, a single thrust
    will suffice. Good night.

III. *The Osprey Suicides*

The Island Drought

Water on four
   sides, we're struck by drought;
the golf course is parched stubble, Sahara-dry.
   Water trucks haul
   liquid tonnage around the clock.
I peer down my hillside as from a tower. Roofs
   of corrugated steel
   catch the sun and hurl it
into my eyes. What falls must be caught, held,
   kept; rain-
   water in the precious gutters
slips into the cistern—affluence in our throats!
   Much, much
   is offered. And there is much
buying and selling. The sermon and outdoors-choir swell
   the loudspeaker:
   sound rolls from the valley
into my house like waves—the Negro spirituals
   salute the White
   Christ! Thanksgiving Sunday.
Terms. No $ down. Cut-rate salvation for Stateside
   Jewry on the hill.
   If I purchase my cast-off Jesus
from Carib-blacks, Holy Rollers hymn U.S. Stars &
   Stripes. My drowned-
   out radio blows its tubes.
I cannot shut off the Word. My maid, on the upstairs
   porch, hallelujahs!
   Her sins of the night before
(weeks, months) fall off her hide like paralyzed lice.
   She expects to burn,
   at the last, but all she knows
of fire (it is much!) makes her secretly desire Hell-hots.
   In pipe dreams, her employer
   roasts to white ash—for a ringside

seat she would gladly inhabit the oven next door. . . .
        In winter heat,
    for months I sit and swim
in the tunnel of mind. Confined to the one level,
        my vertical thoughts
    rising and falling like buckets
in a dry well—no hearty infidel swervings!—
        how can I abide
    these creaking wheels, the noisy
finger-fuckings of the self, without disgust?
        I can hear the effort
    I make over myself, moaning,
and puffing at the rusty crank that runs the pulleys.

Island Trashfires

Christmas: three tourist
liners in port, two more at anchor
in harbor
mouth; the largest,
a city-block long, eight ship-floors

high, triple-smokestacked. This year, jets
rival the old army transports,
three tail engines
rocketing into steep inclines
on takeoff. Hourly,

the Pan Am whisperjets plow furrows in runway
asphalt, motors reversing an air wall,
wingspan extending far over the parallel
service road, fuselage groaning to a stop
on the miniature landing strip.

The airstrip clings to the west
shore, a Band-Aid on a bruised wrist.
Adjacent to the garbage dump (an open sore
that drains the Island's poisons around the clock), old con-
vairs
lift and lower

over trashfires
and the bellies of pedigreed
sharks—pampered, overfed, domesticated.
Inland, chicken-scrawny mongrels
pick about in the rubble for waste morsels.

In a sleep-daze of search,
they meander suicidally into onrush
of traffic. . . . One airless hot night,

I drive to the airport road's unpaved dead end,
a skipping-stone's hurl

to the triple juncture
of water, runway and fainting bonfire.
Our hideaway fumes carrion-stink.
My carnivore hand swings
to fetch you, huddled

against your door.
In the lowered
headlamps, a three-legged terrier,
favoring its bandaged
stump, spots a tidbit just over the edge,

bobbing in shallows. The mutt
aims a short hop. We see a mako's lifted snout
jerk shut—the twitching furball, headless
in air, falls to the surface. . . .
Vagrant drayhorses

and mules—no crops to plow,
no carts to haul—
are sold for children's sport, or abandoned
in backwoods. They drift over untilled farmland,
straying into paths of semis,

diesels. . . . One morning, a half-starved donkey,
emaciated, is found roped to a tree, three arrows piercing
his belly; still alive on his feet, suffering
noiselessly; in his eyes,
absence, a luminous void. At the hairpin

curve, on the main drag to Island Top Mountain,
the overturned cement truck
lies smoking. Alongside the buckled hood,
a gray-and-white flecked
roan mare, legs splayed like old pipe cleaners under her
bloated

abdomen, soaks in a pool of motor oil and blood.
A block or two below, a man about seventy,
with great, burl-knuckled hands, motions passing cars
to stop. The drivers, fierce-eyed, look away
from the poor whitetrash master

mechanic; southern expatriate from Tulsa
in faded cloud-pale blue
coveralls, he carries the secret of pure failure
("Failed brakes!") from car to car, curled in immaculate
vast hands like a jewel. . . . Easter:

dawn traffic, slowed to a crawl—
no chance to pass on the serpentining downgrade—
bottlenecks. Midway on Rappune Hill,
the she-goats, their twitching hindquarters upraised
into motorists' faces,

thrust their narrow jaws
through gaps in fence wire. With languorous
tobacco-chawing sideways chops and grinds, they munch
the roadside clover, and won't be budged.
A ninety-year-old Anguillan,

the goat-boy, wags his pole at the stalled nannies.
As if dancing the tango
or conducting a minuet,
his arms, caressive and slow,
undulate.

Huntington Beach

Terraces of oil-pumps, like swarms
Of grasshoppers harnessed in garden chain gangs,
Line the highway. Across the road, bathers,
At civilized and private intervals,
Cluster. They challenge the lusty breakers of the shore
On flying flakes and lacerate the surf
With shark-like fins.

Some, their backs
To the water,
Propped on canvas hinges
(at four adjustable angles to the horizontal),
Admire the opulent palms, hedges, ivies
That camouflage the orchard miles of swinging derricks,
Sucking dry the bowels of the sea.

The labyrinth of pipelines,
Ubiquitous,
Like networks of gopher-tunnels undermining lawns,
Stretches for tens of miles, miles under the sea-floor.
Somewhere, a bather puts his ear to the classical seashell.
In place of the familiar resonance,
A dissonant air-drill.

Hotel Morgue of Miami Beach

The natives act like tourists
in this playground for the sportive rich.
Cruising from newer Collins to old,
and back, is the queerest
tour I've taken. The long-finned batch
of Cadillacs give over to box-shaped
limousines, old Fleetwoods, hearses. Drivers bald
and hatless succeed prim chauffeurs.
Leopard-skin seat-covers replace old leather—and velvet-
    draped
windows, screening women who frequent coiffeurs.

The day I arrive, I am duty-
bound to visit the newest hotel.
Just open a week, it has lost its charm
for some. The chatty
local set stampede like cattle
through block-long ballrooms, lobbies,
testing the silence of rugs, whether lampshades be firm
enough. I hover in an archway,
dizzy from dramatic heights withindoors. This palace
soon will join the hotel mortuary.

Mile upon mile of darkening
stucco, I circuit *old* high-class hangouts.
Corpse-hotels date about nineteen-hundred.
Fallen plaster, a crumbling
porch-ledge, involve me. The present blacks out.
Kept up by my grandfather's hand,
these ruins, he left, from his coin-purse heart are sundered.
Through jagged cracks in a wall,
blank faces stare. Apparitional, my rheumy-eyed grandfather motions me back with a tender claw.

63

The Professionals

. . . *for they had contracted
American dreams. . . .*

—Louis Simpson

1. Ph.D.

He has layers and layers of pages
tucked under his skin—
brain cells circulate in his lymph like oxygen.

He tunnels through the long libraries of night.
The knives and forks of his eyes
dismember

thousands of minuscule syllable-lives, limb from limb
and joint by joint,
picking the sentences clean like chicken bones.

There are teeth in the thighs of bindings—
a permanent bite. And the swellings will never go down.
His perfect memory scoops out the delicate flesh
       of paragraphs

like testicles from a scrotum.
In dreams, he fondles the disembowelled centuries
like so many pet spaniels.

2. Real Estater

Our handshake
shifts, my hand
a doorknob
turning in his grip.

64

In his eyes, a door keeps
slamming shut;
behind his smile,
a key twists
in a dark lock.

His handkerchief
spreads like a welcome
mat, too white
to be true, a flag
or a mask.

       Wherever
he stays, or looks,
for sale lurks.
He will lease my
undug grave
to bones in search
of a bed . . .

      He sleeps
in my telephone
wire. At his touch,
the doorbell shrieks.

The Mountain Hoax

(San Bernardino, California)

I smell mountain
overhead. The snow-cap
breathes a way
of its own and leaves
icy traces
in the lower air.
On clear (there are some
such) days,
I am told the mountain
is visible (60–
70) miles
in the distance. Up close,
it haunts the local
residents, seeming
to loom on all sides
at once. The casual
driver is so taxed
(unknowingly) by the effort
to resist its beauties,
he finds he must halt
the car or risk
a collision. On all
four sides the windows
are met by cliff,
its foliage and rock
formations so stark
they capture the eye,
utterly. This day
in December, I
have only my memory
of local soft-
sell lore and a faint

twinge of the nostrils
to remind me that any
mountain exists
nearby. No fog
ever cuts into corneas
like this, nor leaves
so many layers
of blur-film so fast
on even door-windows.
You can hardly drive
a freeway-mile
before day appears
dusk, no help
from headlights. Spot-
lessly clean the moment
after wiping, no view
is visible, much
beyond the shoulder,
in full day-glare.
The verysightof so
much dirt-soaked air
leaves the strong of lungs
gasping for breath
and squinting back tears
as few sandstorms
in the desert exact.
An infrequent flash
of light on the foothills,
an occasional royal
palm thrusting
over the motorists
from the roadside planter-
space coaxes
me to remember what
State I am in,
what coast I am near,
what cold I have left
behind . . . but the cost, in
sight, weighs most.

The First Light

Cold with a special crispness,
        this morning
        aches to reveal
its wonders. The shock is so sudden
        I can hardly
        trace, for a moment,

what moves me so. Squinting
        to catch
        with the eye that magic
which captured the heart in an unheeding
        moment,
        I try *to see*,

to look close at what I'm seeing,
        struck
        first by this tree,
these wires, the way they cut
        through leaves
        and limbs like a saw,

how they lean on mahogany barn
        like strings
        on a sepia violin,
and hum with a low, clear sound
        as a light wind
        quivers their tautness.

I widen my perspective to include
        the cloudless
        skyscape. Birds
twitch through resistless air.
        If I lift
        my finger, I swear

68

I can touch their wings, without pressing
             feathers.
        If I concentrate hard,
I can fasten all swooping birds
             to the cliff-
        face miles behind them.

The skyline, a mismade chain saw
             warped
        to edge the horizon,
is serrated with peaks in unbroken
             progression,
        and I find myself

craning my neck in a full circle
             to hunt
        for an exit from so much
shark-toothed rock, and find none,
             dizzy
        with repeated turning,

no checkpoint to start or stop at.
             By degrees,
        my baffled eye
settles on available landmarks:
             a vine
        or roads, winding

in a delicate spiral to the sky,
             sun-flash
        on a drifting car-
roof, a ring of pine-tops, lining
             a stretch
        of horizon like a row

of spears, stark as charred match-
             sticks . . .
        and I'm shaken with awe.
Where has the gauze-air vanished?
             The light
        has changed its colors.

It has been the first rain in ten
months,
I, the first man,
surveying a light of creation.
I am back
where all things begin.

The Osprey Suicides

> *Occasionally, an osprey locks its talons into a fish*
> *too large to handle and is pulled under to drown.*
>
> —Roger Tory Peterson

1. *Samurai: Suicides of the South*

Casting from the Miami causeway
   near Key Biscayne,
     not a nibble
for hours into the sultry dawn (nor a scant gust,
   no faint wind-whiffles),
my last tackle lost to heavy current and the bottom-
      snags, I
   empty the bucket
of live bait—squirming ten-legged shrimp—
       lean over the concrete guardrail, and stare
      into the water below. A blurred
     shadow, flashing, rises from the depths;
     distorted by its violent whirring,
the image seems oddly close to, as if
   somehow above, the surface—
     a ghostfish.
Now it hovers in one spot, halts, appears to settle
   on the surface, stationary
but for a checkered dazzle of black-and-white splotches
     blending
   with the pale gray-white
reflection of the bridge—all image!

     All's a mirroring, I think, as a soft
    rhythmic swishing overhead
      twists my neck in an abrupt upward reflex.
    I'm arrested—checked and held—
  by a brilliant osprey (the exact

twin of the mirrored
　　water-blur)
suspended on laboring wings, transfixed, as if impaled
　　on a fifty-foot pole.
Then he plunges headlong, leaving me staring into vacancy.
　　My eyes,
　　two arrows streaking
　for the target, race his plumb-line descent.
　　　　　　He strikes the water—talons thrown forward
　　　on long white legs extended
　　　　like pitchforks—the only visible prey
　　　is his own unblurred mirror-double:

　the two birds, bilaterally symmetrical,
　　　collide, melting into
　　　each other:
both ospreys explode in foam! The powerful wingbeats
　　breaking his dive
churn the surface into a wall of spray that hides all
　　　but outermost
　　wingtips and beak
held aloft, head never submerged.
　　　　The wings, never folded, madly quicken,
　　　working ferociously for lift-off,
　　　　as the bird slowly emerges from the cloak
　　of foam—airborne at last—
clutching a large red snapper
　in his curled talons,
　　his burden
losing drag, approaching weightlessness, while he gains
　　　speed and altitude.
　　　　　　As he straightens
　　into a vertical ascent,
　his water-image dims and shrinks,

　　　while a matching sky-image above, hanging
　　　immobile like a lantern projection
　　　　on the cloudscape, awaits his swift approach.
　　Grown distrustful of optic

72

fakes, I blink my eyes in wonder. . . .
   I look again.
As the climbing osprey diminishes in size, his perfected
   sky-twin, unshrinking,
glides in a slow circle on extended wings. Before the lower
    bird meets
  his soul-brother in heaven,
 the upper bird swoops down from above,
     declaring himself a piratical bald eagle.
    Trying to catch the osprey unawares,

 the eagle homes in on him
   and executes
a precision-timed swipe at the snapper. The smaller bird,
   screaming his outrage,
swerves at the last possible instant, easily dodging clear
   without halting—
  or even appreciably
 slowing—his rate of ascension.
    The emperor of birds,
    infuriated, soars quickly above the osprey,
    again and again, whose masterful
side-veerings always deftly elude
  the eagle dive-bomber's
   aerial thrusts
as both raptors, hurtling like runaway kites into the upper
   air,
  are finally reduced
to little more than speckled motes against the sky. The osprey,
   straining
  to lift his freightage, climbs
 slower and slower; his outleaps

    grow fiercer; but at last
   he drops the fish. The eagle, plummeting,
    intercepts the falling carcass
  just before it reaches the sea;
   he glides
a few feet above sea level, flaunting his prize. Morning

trade winds arising,
I spot the osprey scanning the gusty bay
for surface game.
Following his search,
I notice a spread-winged highflier—
misidentified earlier
as obscure cloud-mirage—
now rapidly descending; he coasts

on motionless, vast, dark wings
outspread. Squinting
at the frigatebird's
unmistakable forked tail and webbed feet, I hardly notice
his side-slipping maneuvers
into position over the bald eagle. One savage pounce—
a bone-breaking
peck!—and his long
hooked beak instantly hijacks
the limp fish from the eagle's surprised claws,
old baldy bested by the man-of-war bird,
master of sky-to-sea pirates. The frigate
never alights on the water:
despite his onetime
water-strutting
webbed feet—now shrunken and held close to his body
on legs shortened
for total streamlining—he is unable to rise
from the sea
once fallen. The eagle
haltingly cruises downwind,

a dazed prince of the air drifting earthward.
The osprey keeps wending upward and outward, his
wings
a weft in the wind's shuttle,
his body lofted in broader circles
of a slowly upwinding
spiral.
He traces the periphery of an inverted cone with apex
near the bay's center,

74

extending his range of surface-tracking radar;
  gauging
 all points below
at once, he surveys a commanding
    view of a great plain of water stretching
   from shore to shore. Checking
    himself at about one-hundred feet, he hovers—
   a bombardier sighting his target—

and drops like a discharged projectile.
  The shower of spray,
   bubbling
higher and higher over the flapping wings, froths
  like a small geyser
 as the bird struggles to hoist
   the payload
   tugging him under.
 The towering spume lowers, deflates,
     when a blast of wind sucks his exposed wing
          ends
    and hurls him high over the swells
 hefting a yards-long thick garfish,
   violently
whipping about, bending its wiry silverflanks double upon
  the talons piercing
 its back. As the osprey levels off,
  he coasts on a line
 parallel to the surface, perhaps five

     wingspans high. The strong head wind shifts
   course and fades; the osprey
     pivots to catch the last of the wind; wind
    dying, he surges nose-upward
 on strenuously heaving wingflaps,
  his claws buried
   in the gar's
spine, and sinking deeper, the fish jerking its tail in its
   last
   shimmering death throes.

I drop my eyes to the pair mirrored below, the reflected
        battle-
    thrashing of bird and prey
  strangely altered by optical alchemy
                into the amorous writhings of mating lovers,
            the upper figure alternately lifting,
                and being pulled down by the lower; but fol-
                    lowing
            a peak of vigorous flailing

  all motion quavers to a stillness.
    Before I can lift
        my eyes back
to the aerial pair, the aquatic pair has swallowed the origi-
    nal
        as echo drinks up sound.
    The osprey, collapsing on outstretched
            wings, falls
        into its image, still hugging
  its victim and slaughterer to its breast.

                2. *DDT: Suicides of the North*

    Bird lovers living near the Connecticut River estuary
            connecting with Long Island Sound
  erect cart wheels atop poles to lure survivors
      of the dwindling osprey colony.
                                A few mating pairs
            oblige, finding the wheels'
  rotted hubs and spokes apt support
        for the great heavy nests of sticks.
                            Bird-watcher's
                                report.
            Grim news from next door eyries.
  Hatchlings, down seven-eighths. Egg-layings,
        normal. Offset by mysterious egg disappearances.
        Chief suspect: poacher raccoons.
  Ruled out by failure of raccoon-proof nesting
        platforms. Females observed sitting on unhatched eggs
            for seventy days, twice the normal

    76

gestation period—still, no brood.

Months pass.

Bizarre symptoms reported.

Conjectured DDT-onset
of hastened

senility.

Or osprey insanity.

Three foreign objects turn up in one nest:
a child's rubber ball, a cracked golf ball, a rainbow-
colored, decorative glass egg;
the nest's absent matron, returning with a near-oval
bleached white sea snail shell locked in her talons,
settles down for a five-week roost
on her new miscellaneous hatchery.

Outage!—
across the river. An all-night freak power failure,
darkening all homes along the river's
north bank.

At daybreak, the power-and-light
inspector, hunting the fault, locates an upturned
corrugated metal trash can cover
(half-fallen from the crossbars of a power pole onto short-
circuited wires) containing a nest of large sticks, three
unbroken
osprey eggs, and a puddle of rain water
that tipped the innovatory eyrie during the night's
downpour.

Commonly, osprey mates choose a deserted
island for nesting sites.

One mating couple is observed migrating inland
from an ideally hidden eyrie on a dead spruce snag,
stranded on Great Island by storm tides,
to build a pole nest at a busy traffic intersection;
another pair abandons an island nest for a poletop site
beside the railroad tracks, and develop
a preternatural immunity to the clatter and roar
of the passing express.

A lone, unseasonable bald eagle,
paying an early visit from the north
country, long before the first ice floes form

on the river, gliding high over the Great Island nesting
                territory,
            is harried from above by a daredevil
shrieking male osprey swooping again and again
        toward his heftier imposing cousin as if trying to drive
                him
            out of violated private air space—
both birds augustly silhouetted against the sky,
        hundreds of feet above all nests.
                                    The eagle, making a few
            tame feints, hardly bothering to flinch
or fight back, resumes his former course of drift,
        soaring and coasting effortlessly away from the attacker.
        Moments later, the militant osprey
slowly drops on five-foot-wide extended wings
        to his oak-limb nest, bearing a two-pound gray mullet
                in both claws, with its head
half-eaten away.
                        Still nibbling as he alights,
        osprey-sire, sole provider for the nesting young,
                oddly withholds his catch
from three famished nurslings—ignoring their clucks
        and the mother's strident screaming—and continues
                to munch
            laterally across the body and into the tail,
as if deaf to their rising chorus of squawks.

The Skeletonizers

1

Two priests,
living on opposite sides of the Rio
Araguaia, love
to bathe
in the river: the protestant missionary—
a northland wayfarer—
and the native
catholic padre matching opposite faiths
and birthrights against
death's
smalljawed disembowellers. Both
have been nicked and gouged,
bled closer
to the truth. Both, panicked, have fled
the wound-trickled banquet,
the blood-letting
witch's broth in the devil's kitchen
of their own heart's soup.
Both
have outswum the delicious weepings
that oozed from leaks
in their cleft
body-dikes. Both, scabbed and scarring,
return every day
to the river.

2.

No raft or primitive dugout between them (a hollowed-out log,
once a navigable boat,
lies stranded on shore,
its bottom—rotted and gaping—upturned, as if awaiting
repairs),

the two men of the cloth
who have never met
wave fraternal daily greetings across one hundred feet
of sluggish chocolate-
brown crosscurrents.
One foggy morning,
the young clergymen—a fullbearded Oklahoman exile of three
years service
to river Indians—
awakens to a clatter
of howls and shouts from a midriver fracas. Scuffling from
his thatched
cottage to the riverbank,
he peers through mangrove
fronds and overhanging thickets of roots into impenetrable
mist.
As the wails subside
to a volley of rhythmic
grunts and splashings, a single tortured face cuts through
the dusk,
its short grizzled beard
and furrowed cheeks
bobbing between wildly flailing arms, limbs employed less
as paddles
than hammers, cudgeling
the mirror-calm surface.
When the figure nears shore, the dazed priest beholds several
red-bellied
nattereri leaping
vertically out of the water,
their jaws snapping like hedge clippers, all wheeling about
on their tails,
somersaulting in air,
revolving in orbits narrowly
encircling the swimmer. A scene flashes into the young
divine's memory
from a film of piranha
carnage viewed in childhood—
a grisly simmering and boiling of the surface over the sub-

merged victim
    signalled the most advanced
    stages of skeletonizing. The youth
plunges into the churning melee, seizes his elder fellow
    divine under both arms,
      swiftly tows him to shore
      in a welter of lightweight
fierce-mouthed trolls—those aquariumsized angry freshwater
    elves—
      and flings him, a forked turnip
      of waterlogged driftwood,
a few yards up the sloped bank. Braced on elbow-stiffened
    poles of his arms,
      he vaults his long trunk upward,
      hefting his lower body
ashore, clear of those greedy nippers and shearers. The tan-
    gled hulk
      opposite slowly unfolds
      and staggers to its feet,
spraying thin streams of red—a dozen absurd fountains and
    one little spurting
      neck-geyser. Advancing
      a few steps, the old Spaniard
raises a bronzed hand jetting from two gashed finger-stumps,
    deftly plucks
      a weathered tobacco pouch
      from his stout liana waistband,
takes a pinch of the dampened tobacco, wads it into a ball,
    and squeezes it
      into a neck-wound; then passes
      the crinkled leather purse
to his comrade. Silence. Wordless communion. All in one mo-
    tion, a mad flapping
      of hands, hands
    flying wildly about like mating geese;
        how many hands?—two,
      four, six?—
    hands coming together, hands streaking
        apart, hands ripping
    both shirts

from their backs and tearing them into strips,
          hands pressing tobacco-plugs
     into sockets,
hands patching deep notches in thighs,
          wounds like mouths
     in hips,
flanks, scooped-out hollows in buttocks;
          hands tying each poultice
     firmly in place,
tobacco cleansing and binding. The cupped
          hands loop and swing,
     curvetting
like humped-up, arch-backed stallions,
          leaping and mending,
     dancing
and healing, faster and faster, hands
          light as butterfly's
     wings
vanishing, at last, in a wound-kissing
          blood-stanched blur. . . .
     Angel-hands
swept in a surgical dance of bandaging,
          a wound-dresser's dance
     of caressings,
a flutter-dance of wrappings and windings,
          a dance of mummywound
     handblessings.

3.

Quiescence. All the blood-spouts stoppered, young Peter,
          covered with Ramon's
     caking gore, sits and listens
     to the elder's chanted recital:
"We two rivermates, who are more than brothers, our two
          bloods spilled
     by the seafaced rodents—
     half whiskerless pack rats,
half scalyskinned furless mini-wolves, our systole-diastole
          pumped lifestreams

82

mixing over and over, becalmed
in the steadier mainstream currents
of the paternal Rio Araguaia; though we have never touched
hands, never met
in the flesh before this day,
we two, I say, are mated
forever in the river—our church, our baptismal, our altar
—who wear the stigmata
of our wedded spirits, the lifelong
toothscalpeled tattoos, U.S.
silverdollarsized fleshscooped brands, gashed and notched
in our manly limbs. . . .
Our bodies are survival maps,
the scars,
a geography of battles
won, death outwitted, bite by bite, in a contest
of holes and fillings; gaps
and gouges
stuffed with scar-growths
furious as tumors or fetuses, the body a manyheaded
hydra which mocks endless decapitations
by growing back
two heads for one!
Under every head lost, two others, two others;
the body a starfish which mocks
endless
amputations by regrowing
severed limbs; under every arm lost another,
another, and within arms lost
other
whole stars, whole stars.
The body trains and trains for its immortal quarrel
with death's dollfaced fish persuaders.
The body
divests afterbirths
of chomped fleshlumps; the body begets newbirths:
its tough scarpocks argue back, argue
rebirths against
the munched invective
of death's steeltrapjawed articulators and utterers,

83

against the swelling biceps of tiny
          jaw-muscles—
               those savage Japanese
miniatures—that work the machinesaws of triangular-
     knived small mouths; the body matching
          its whole-oval
               fullmoon scars
against those razor-sprocketed halfmoons of the mouth—
     the uppers and lowers—of death's choppers
          and snippers,
               of death's defleshers.
In the dreamlife of tissues, amputees rejoice,
     amputees dance mockeries of death.
          In the body's
               long dream, armies
of skins, armies of babysmooth scarskins, dance
     mockeries of death. Under the river,
          under the dark
               flowing dream of the rivergod's
long sleep, the hurt body learns, the body wounded
     unwounds, the body winded, unwinds
          a wisdom
               of tough scarskins."